Common Sense Supervision

(A Practical Survival Guide)

By David R. Cooley

Introduction

Thirty years! That's a long time to stay with any one company anymore. It's almost unheard of. I am one of the lucky ones that hitched my wagon to a great company right out of high school and hopefully will retire with that same company when I reach my 40 year mark. As cliché' as it sounds, times are different. Companies don't seem to hold on to people quite so long and employees don't seem to stay with companies as long. Everybody's always looking for the greener pasture.

I started with my company on the ground floor as a furnace operator on a galvanizing line and was quickly promoted to a line supervisor. I was attending Northwood University, working 50 to 60 hours a week and trying to raise a family. I was green and trying to learn fast. I worked very hard and learned as much as I could as quickly as I could. That finally paid dividends when I was offered my own brand new plant to start up and run. As I continued my career there were many times that I wished I had a good survival guide to help me through the rough patches. That's why I decided to write this book. I want to help new supervisor candidates by sharing my knowledge and giving some good, sound practical advice.

That's really all this book is… some good old fashion, sound common sense and practical advice.

I have read a lot of good books by a lot of great authors that have helped me along my journey. I got the most value from the shorter, straight to the point books such as "Who Moved My Cheese." Anyone that knows me knows that I have very little patience. Not a good trait to have when supervising people. I was always aware that I was impatient and tried hard not to let it be my downfall. Because of my intolerance or lack of patience I would have a hard time getting a book to hold my attention. I was never one to read long novels. Supervisor and Managers don't often have a lot of free time; so shorter, more to the point books make better sense.

While I truly was green and lacking real life experience, I was honestly born to be a leader. I knew this was my destiny from a very young age. I remember being tested in the 6th grade and the feedback said that I would be a leader of some sort. My college knowledge mixed with skills that I knew were very important helped guide my path. I don't mean to over simplify things but if you want to be a good supervisor, follow the basic common sense rules that we learned as a child…

- *LISTEN TO OTHERS, SERIUOUSLY...LISTEN!*
- *ADMIT TO MAKING MISTAKES AND DON'T BE AFRAID TO ASK FOR HELP*
- *TREAT OTHERS THE WAY THAT YOU WOULD WANT TO BE TREATED*
- *BE HONEST, FAIR AND CONSISTENT*
- *WHEN YOU SAY YOU ARE GOING TO DO SOMETHING, DO IT!*
- *REMEMBER THAT WE ARE ALL JUST PEOPLE BUT WE HAVE DIFFERENT PERSONALITIES*
- *RESPECT THE RIGHTS AND SPACE OF OTHERS*

Sounds pretty simple, right? Well, if you follow the simple rules and don't sway, the rest of the stuff will come. Problems arise when you start to create "grey" areas and stop being consistent. Most employees just want to be heard and they want to be treated fairly. Now, of course you will always have those individuals that are never happy and just come in every day miserable. Remember that that's their issue and all that you can do it stay consistent, try to help and listen and give them the tools they need to do their job.

Remember, there is a huge difference between being a boss and being a leader. Anybody can shout out orders. There's no need to raise your voice, or act like you are better than anyone else. We are all on the same team with the same goals, be a leader and mentor, not a "boss man".

I hope this book helps some future or current supervisors in some way. Supervision can be very humbling. It comes with a tremendous amount of responsibility but also repercussions. You are responsible for the safety and well-being of your employees. You can be held accountable in a court of law if you ignore safety policies or unsafe conditions! When you are made aware of an unsafe situation or a complaint such as discrimination, you have a responsibility to handle that situation properly and report it to the appropriate people.

Use common sense, do the right thing and
never be afraid to ask for help. The worst decision
that decision that a supervisor can make is NO
decision!

CHAPTER ONE

SAFETY FIRST

Whether you are new to supervision or a seasoned veteran, safety should always be your top priority. It has to be the first and most important thought of the day. If your top management does not make safety a top priority, you may be working for the wrong company. Safety is a culture and should be a core value at every company.

Fortunately, I have never witnessed a severe injury or death. That's pretty significant when you consider that I work in the steel industry. I have witnessed many near misses and first aid type injuries and a few bad ones. I am thankful that I never had to call a spouse with the daunting news that her husband was severely injured or worse.

I think the key is you MUST have buy in from the very top of the chain. If you don't have support to build and enforce a safety program, you will not be successful. Like any house or structure, you have to have a sturdy foundation. From PPE to Lock Out / Tag Out, you must have defined safety rules and employees must be held accountable to follow them. You must have buy-in from the top, though. You can spend years building the right program, but when the CEO comes strutting

through the plant without his safety glasses on...
you just killed your safety program.

Be involved in all aspects of safety. Make
sure to have hourly employees involved in the
process. Every facility should have a sound safety
committee and ideally should have sub-
committee's branching from there. Every facility
should have a written safety program, evacuation
plan, JSA's (Job Safety Analysis) and a proactive
approach to safety. Each year your facility should
write a safety incident reduction plan with clear
goals to reduce or eliminate recordable accidents,
incidents and near misses.

In the unfortunate event of an accident,
incident or near miss a good supervisor will record
all pertinent information immediately and fill out
an incident report. A good incident report should
include the following...

- ➢ Date and time of event.
- ➢ Exact details of how the event happened.
- ➢ Witness statements.
- ➢ Statement from the individual involved.
- ➢ Immediate containment measures.
- ➢ Get plenty of documentation and pictures.

Remember, the purpose of a good incident investigation is to prevent reoccurrence. Within 24 hours of an incident, you should gather a team to review the incident and complete a corrective action form. Your team should be cross functional with supervision and hourly employees. Perform root cause analysis and devise a plan to ensure such an event cannot be repeated.

Use common problem solving techniques such as "5 WHY", fishbone diagrams etc. Remember to break the issue down to separate categories such as MAN, METHOD, MACHINE, or MATERIAL. Always try to mistake proof the issue from happening again. The best corrective action is engineering in a solution rather than adding external steps or personal protective equipment. Never rely on employees to follow the rules. You have to take away the potential failures. A good corrective action digs deep and doesn't use terms like "employee error" or "it was just a mistake". Yes, it's called an accident, but you can bet that it was avoidable.

A good example...

Johnny was working by a running machine and inspecting the product. He noticed a defect and not thinking, reached to touch the product to better understand what the defect was. The product running on the machine cut his finger, requiring seven stitches. After the incident investigation, management instituted a new rule that everybody had to wear gloves before touching any product. Here is a better long term solution… the engineering group installed and programed a light curtain to automatically stop the line if any employee reached in to touch the product. This mistake proofing removes the accidental poor judgment call from the equation. Always provide mistake proof measures when possible.

Always stay on top of safety and be proactive. At least once a week, do a thorough walkthrough with a checklist looking for unsafe conditions such as…

- Fire extinguishers
- Eye wash stations
- Exit lights and signs
- Exit doors not blocked
- Guarding in place
- Trip hazards
- Housekeeping concerns
- Oil on the floor
- Forklift safety and employees wearing seat belts

- ➢ Employees wearing proper PPE
- ➢ Extension cords to code not under rugs or mats
- ➢ Flammables stored properly
- ➢ Proper warehouse stacking of materials
- ➢ Environmental concerns such as leaking hydraulic fluid
- ➢ Open electrical cabinets
- ➢ Fire hazards (debris piled up)

It's always a good idea to have a third party spend a day with your safety team doing a safety walkthrough and inspection. Sometimes you can't see the forest through the trees. A new set of eyes can be a very useful tool. If you have a good relationship with another company, it might be a good idea to meet with them a few times a year to brainstorm and benchmark. Share ideas and do wall to wall walkthroughs with each other. Always stay up to date with the OSHA rules and perform yearly training as required. Rules vary by state but it is important to train to the following subjects as a minimum...

- ➢ Right to Know (Global Harmonization)
- ➢ Lock Out Tag Out
- ➢ Confined Space

- PPE Requirements
- Forklift and Crane safety and certification
- Blood Bourne Pathogens
- Hazardous Waste handling
- Fire Safety
- Machine Guarding

All accidents are avoidable. Some people say that they are not and that's why they call them accidents. If you break it down however, you will find that there is always an underlying factor that led to or contributed to the event. You have to start with the right culture and mindset. Every employee needs to be thinking safety not only on the job, but at home as well. Always encourage employees to bring any unsafe condition or unsafe act to your attention immediately. Have a system to report unsafe conditions or unsafe acts anonymously. Empower all employees with the right and responsibility to stop an unsafe act.

If you have buy in from the top, a safety culture that everyone is on board with and a management staff that will provide all of the tools needed to ensure a safe environment; then you are more than half way there. Try to involve employees with incentives, contests or newsletters. Keep safety in the face of your employees every day.

Don't be a company that has a slogan that says "SAFETY FIRST". Be the company that walks, breathes and lives safety EVERY DAY! It has to be the first priority, it has to be a core value and everybody has to take ownership. Be that leader that promotes safety and leads by example. Ask your employees…"Is there anything that you are doing that you don't feel 100% safe doing"? Show your employees your sincerity and your actions to provide a safe workplace.

Lead by example…

Remember the safety incident triangle. Learn from near misses, don't discard them. Often the difference between a near miss and a fatality is dumb luck or timing. Statistically, for every 600 near misses, there is a severe injury or a fatality. You will find that his data rings true thorough most industries.

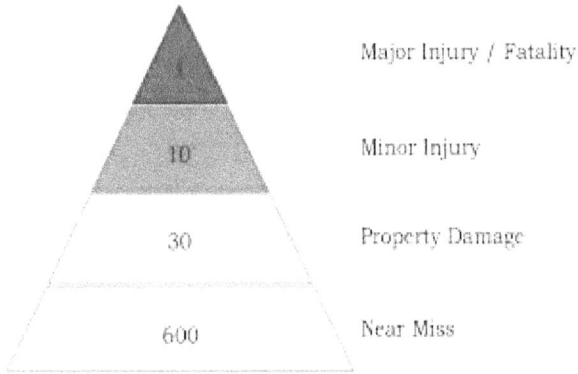

Major Injury / Fatality

Minor Injury

Property Damage

Near Miss

CHAPTER TWO

WE ARE ALL JUST PEOPLE

I have found that one of the toughest adjustments for a new supervisor is dealing with many different personalities. Sometimes you need to take a step back and remember that we are all just people; but we are all very different. What may make John happy might not work for Kevin. While Fred may perceive a decision made by a supervisor to be favoritism, Andy may view the situation as discrimination.

Whether real or perceived, favoritism is a huge concern and must be dealt with swiftly. It will become a cancer. Always treat everybody the same and eliminate grey areas. If possible, take the employee out of the equation and replace them with a family member. You do not want to subconsciously treat a less than stellar employee differently than a great employee.

Instead, always deal with the facts. Respond to the situation and be consistent no matter who the employee. You may find yourself leaning toward discipline simply because you don't necessarily care for an employee or the employee is average at best. Treat everybody the same. You need to address particular acts separately. If you have a sub-par employee, you need to coach and counsel this employee to try and make them more productive.

If an employee just doesn't get with the program or shows no improvement, it is time to start documenting specific actions and follow your company progressive discipline policy. Nobody ever wants to terminate an employee but unfortunately the reality is that there are times when it needs to be done. Remember… You don't fire poor performing employees, they fire themselves. Give them every opportunity to meet the standards that are required of them. Make sure that they have all of the tools needed to be successful. If they still can't perform, then it is time to replace them with somebody that can.

It has been said that a supervisor will spend 80% of his time on 20% of the workforce. In my 30 years of experience, I have absolutely found this to be true. You can work hard to hire the best candidates, but eventually the bad apples will infiltrate and you will be spending a great deal of time working out issues with these people. They are never happy no matter what you do.

These employees are the ones that complain they are working too much overtime and a month later complain they aren't getting enough overtime and can't feed their families. You will find them to always be negative and bad mouthing the company or management. The best way to combat these individuals is with facts. Always be completely honest and open with them. Never let yourself get into an argument with them; stick to the facts and be very diplomatic.

You really want to always be honest with all of your employees anyway. Don't ever sugar coat issues or hope that problems will just go away. Sometimes it's hard delivering bad news, but a good supervisor sometimes has to do this. When you do deliver bad news, do not ever push all the blame to upper management. I have worked with supervisors that communicate with their employees saying things like…"I certainly don't agree with them, but corporate wants us to do…." This scapegoat mentality is not professional.

Simply deliver the message. "Guys, we are not going to have a company picnic this year". "We just haven't been profitable as of late and the budget won't allow it". "Maybe next year" is a much better approach than… "Those jerks say there isn't any money for a company picnic this year. What a load of crap." You may feel like you are bonding with your group and backing them, but that's not what a good supervisor does.

A supervisor's main responsibility is communicating effectively. It is very important to be a great listener. You need to be able to successfully communicate both directions. It is vital for a good supervisor. It needs to be said to not do the opposite either. Do not report to management... "Those whinny babies want to know why there's no picnic this year". Be professional. Everybody deserves your respect. You may not get the respect that you think you deserve, but make sure that you always give the utmost respect to everyone that you deal with. Respect should be earned, especially when you are a supervisor.

It's always a good idea to avoid confrontational topics such as politics and religion. Although it is certainly your right as an American, it's an area that can cause ill feelings. Everybody has an opinion and many people are very passionate about their opinions. Best to steer clear in this area. No sense in opening a can of worms, a supervisor has enough on his plate without causing more drama.

It will be harder to earn respect if you come up through the ranks. Many a potential supervisor will find themselves in an awkward situation making the transition. Guys on the production floor that were your friends will try to take advantage of you. Some people will think that you didn't deserve the promotion and maybe felt that they were more qualified. They will certainly have a chip on their shoulder. Stay with the plan and treat everybody the same. If you are fair and consistent and treat others with respect, eventually you will earn their respect. Remember, some people do not have a firm grasp on reality. I have had many people ask to be considered for an opening in supervision that do not have a clue. They honestly feel that they are the best candidate though.

Everybody has life issues. Most of the time you don't know if somebody is having marital problems, health issue with them or a family member, financial problems... Whatever the case may be, we are all human and everyday issues that we have to deal with. Employees need to be focused and leave their personal lives at the door, but at the same time we need to have compassion and be available to communicate with them.

Every day will be different and filled with challenges and obstacles. Try to take one day at a time and stick to the facts. Don't let emotions cloud your judgment, be consistent, fair, compassionate and honest at all times.

CHAPTER THREE

ALWAYS FOLLOW THROUGH (And Up)

Speaking from experience, there are few feelings worse than your boss asking you a direct question that he obviously expects a quick and accurate answer to and you really don't know. Of course every boss has a different demeanor and style but I have found that honesty is the best policy. The worst thing you can do in this case is guess. Simply tell your Manager that you need a little time to give the best answer and that you will get them an answer very soon. The important part here is that you follow up immediately. Do not forget.

Most Managers will expect that you should know the answer to the questions that they are asking. Always try to stay proactive and anticipate the questions that will be asked of you. Get to know what is important to your Manager. The obvious questions will normally have to do with safety, quality and productivity. Try to stay in the loop and know your business. It's normally pretty easy to anticipate what your boss needs to know. Be honest, don't guess and make sure you get the answer needed ASAP!

Equally important is getting back to the people that report to you. If an employee has a concern that he is addressing with you, take it seriously. It may not seem significant to you, but most assuredly it is very important to them. Normally, they wouldn't ask if it wasn't important. Carry an IPad or a small notebook at all times. Write things down. Pocket memo recorders are helpful too. As a Plant Manager, I like to carry my IPad because I can easily write or dictate notes. I can also take photos of issues in the plant and e-mail them to my supervisors immediately. I don't think they like it so much...

Communication is the key. You will read this sentence time and time again because it is THE most important aspect of becoming a successful supervisor. The vast majority of personnel issues stem from a lack of communication. Most supervisors fail because of a lack of communication. Any good book related to the subject of supervision will speak of constant communication. It is VITAL! There are so many tools available today to make a supervisors life more easy and organized. I didn't have IPads or IPhones when I started supervising. Take advantage of the technology available. There are plenty of apps to help you communicate and stay organized.

Remember, people normally don't like change. They resist it because they are afraid of the unknown. The best tool to combat change is communication. Show your employees how they will benefit or how the company will benefit. Communicate verbally, electronically, using handouts... whatever it takes. You can't over communicate.

Don't get caught with your pants down. What's the one thing definitely worse than not having an acceptable answer for you bosses question? Telling her that you will get an answer very soon and then dropping the ball. How do you think the conversation will go two days later when you are confronted? That is something I guarantee your supervisor will not forget. It paints a picture that you are unreliable or unresponsive.

Another item worth mentioning... It's ok to take a few seconds and think about your answers. You don't want to blurt out something that you will later regret. I remember a supervisor that worked in my company that was asked a direct question from the Company President. "We can't turn any work away; we need to find a way to store more material". "What is your plan?" Unfortunately, the supervisor blurted out, "There's nothing that can be done, we are at capacity". After the President discussed the situation with the supervisor's boss, (the Plant Manager) they found a way to reorganize the space and gain an additional 25% storage. Unfortunately, this individual chose to "pursue other interests". Hey, that's what the official memo said.

Common sense!!! Follow up, keep your promises, meet your deadlines and don't tell your boss something that you will regret! Remember that you were hired to find solutions.

CHAPTER FOUR

CHANGE IS INEVITABLE

One of my favorite books of all time was written by Spencer Johnson, M.D. This bestselling book is called, "Who Moved My Cheese". What a powerful little book. It sums up the perils of going through change in a cute but effective and realistic manner. The hard truth is that CHANGE HAPPENS. There's no way around it. History has shown that the one thing that remains constant is change.

You may have heard the line if you aren't moving forward; you are moving backwards. There is no status quo. There is no happy and satisfied to stay where we are. Everybody is out to invent the faster and better mouse trap. (No pun intended) Two things stand in our way of change, communication and fear. People are afraid to move out of their comfort zone and are afraid of the unknown. Many times, we just don't have all of the facts to know why change has to happen. Nobody ever assumes that change is a good thing and often times it is. The bottom line is that change is necessary.

Other favorite authors of mine are Kenneth Blanchard, Ph.D. and Robert Fulghum. Another example of common sense writing that millions of up and coming supervisors can relate to. It sounds simple, but so true... Everything I Really Need to Know, I Learned In Kindergarten. We really learn at a very early age that change is inevitable. I think the change for the parents leaving their child at school for the first time is more traumatic than what the kids are going through. Isn't that really what it's all about? It sounds so simple, yet many people struggle with it.

Treat others like you want to be treated, if you break something that doesn't belong to you, replace it. Share, be nice, and respect others. These are simple words to live by. So if you want to talk about change, these are great qualities that everyone should change their lifestyles to. Change into being a better person, with goals and priorities, which will make you a better, more effective supervisor.

Unfortunately, there are individuals that want to make changes for the sake of making changes. If these people are your bosses, go with the flow and make the best of it. You still need to get on board and be part of the solution, even if you don't agree with the direction. In reality change is brought on because of a necessary situation, an opportunity to improve, or a continuous improvement idea. I'm not saying that all are positive, but they all start with that direction in mind. Embrace change, don't be negative.

Change will create a stressful time in anyone's life and everybody handles stress differently. Don't assume others are handling change better, worse or differently. They may appear to be aloof or not care, don't assume.

So, what do you do if you have a supervisor or manager that wants to institute change but you REALLY disagree with the direction and just can't seem to get on board? Don't do anything hasty. Spend at least 48 hours and really try to see the other side. If after serious consideration, you think this is not best for the company, ask your supervisor to explain how this will help the company. Respect the opinion of the person trying to institute change and try to cooperate fully.

Stay positive. Remember, you need to always have the best interest of the company in mind.

<u>Points to remember</u>

- Be aware of your surroundings, don't be caught off guard.
- Recognize the writing on the wall.
- Accept change and move on.
- Be flexible, be positive and don't resist or be negative.
- Change is going to happen whether you are on board or not.
- Communicate with others, lack of communications equals negativity.
- Look at the big picture, have vision, don't be near-sighted.

CHAPTER FIVE

FAVORITISM... REAL OR PERCEIVED

Favoritism, boy can it cause a supervisor trouble. Favoritism can be the downfall of many a good supervisor. Sometimes, you may just want to let somebody know that they did a great job. That's great, tell them so. Be careful however that you are not always praising the same people. Don't praise people in front of others, don't single them out. Just as when forced to discipline, you never want to do so in a group. It's ok to tell the group they did a great job, but never single anyone out for any reason.

Some people are just too shy and don't want the attention. Some others will see another employee being praised and may become resentful. Praise and discipline should always be dealt with privately. It's ok to have programs such as "employee of the month." But that's a little different than praising Bob for a job well done in front of a group. Surely, somebody will immediately be thinking… "What about the job that I did?"

Always treat everybody the same. Be consistent. I guarantee if you write up employee "A: for the same thing that employee "B" did, but did not write up employee "B"; you just treated employees differently. That is favoritism and will cause you a mess of trouble. You need to treat everybody the same. Eliminate grey areas. Keep a log if you need to. This way you can go back and check... how did I handle this situation before? Above all, follow the employee handbook and if you aren't 100% sure, call your HR department or your supervisor for help.

You most likely will just be seeing things a little differently, or forgot what you have done in the past. Sometimes you may react differently because of the mood that you are in. Don't make a hasty decision. Be consistent and make sure that you treat everybody the same.

Others will simply perceive that they are being treated differently because they are not doing their job or pulling their weight. They feel like you are picking on them because you are always coaching them. They refuse to take responsibility and they do not want to be held accountable for their actions. Sure, they are correct that you are spending more time with them trying to get them up to speed. Make sure that they understand the only reason that you have a need to "coach" them is because they simply are not performing.

The bottom line is making sure that you are aware of favoritism and perceived favoritism and address any rumblings of such immediately. It is a serious issue that can lead to a lawsuit. Even non warranted, frivolous lawsuits are no fun.

CHAPTER SIX

BASIC FINANCIALS

EBITDA… Say what? The first time I heard the phrase, I had no idea what they were talking about. I knew it had something to do with making money or making a profit; but that was about it.

Earnings Before Interest Taxes and Depreciation and Amortization. That's a mouthful, right? You really don't need to be an accountant to understand what you need to know from the prospective of a supervisor. EBITDA simply put is an accounting measure calculated using a company's net earnings, before interest expenses, taxes, depreciation and amortization are subtracted. It's a quick snapshot showing whether or not the company is profitable.

The basic terms that you should know as a supervisor are below…

- Accounts Payable – a record of short term invoices or bills.   This is usually supplies, services, parts etc…
- Accounts Receivable – a record of money owed to the company for services provided.
- Balance Sheet – a snapshot of a business financial situation on any particular day.

- Budget – a plan for income and expenditures over a period of time in the future.
- Capital – any asset owned by a company.
- COGS (Cost of goods sold) – direct cost to produce goods or services.
- Credit – agreement to pay later for goods or serviced received today. (Money owed)
- Debit –double entry into a ledger as an asset or expense.
- Default – failure to pay on a loan or money owed.
- Equity – value of ownership, usually by deducting liabilities from assets.
- FIFO – First In First Out (rotate stock, ship what comes in first, out first)
- Fixed Asset – any physical asset used to run a business such as a bulldozer.
- Fixed Cost – a cost not directly attributed to production of goods.
- FOB – Free on Board (Destination that something is shipping to and who is responsible to pay for the freight... FOB destination means that whoever receives the goods is responsible for shipping charges. FOB origin means that whoever ships the material is responsible.)

- Gross Income – Total amount of money earned before deducting expenses.
- Gross Profit – What's left from sales after subtracting direct costs. Also known as net sales.
- Insolvent – when a company cannot pay their current bills.
- Invoice – a document given to a customer requesting payment for goods or services. This is different than a statement.
- Margin – difference between the selling price and the amount of profit. If an item sold for $20 and $2 was profit, the margin is 10%.
- Net Assets – (or net worth) is simply assets minus liabilities.
- Net Income – Money earned after taxes and other deductions are taken out.
- Net Profit – Total gross profit minus expenses.
- Overhead – fixed costs needed to run a business such as rent and utilities.
- Variable cost – costs that change depending on the quantity of what is produced.

It may get confusing so try to keep it simple. Control the things that you are responsible for such as manufacturing supplies, shipping supplies, and utilities. Think of it as if you were spending your own money. Make sure there is little or no waste being created unnecessarily.

Overtime is a big area where you can save some money. It is also an area that is normally watched and scrutinized closely. Perform lean exercises such as Value Stream Maps and fine tune your processes. Cross train your workers so that you can have more flexibility if somebody calls off. Keep working at it. Save seconds in the process that lead to minutes and hours.

Proactive preventive maintenance can help save costs by catching a small problem before it turns into a bigger problem. Learn your machinery; listen to the sounds that it makes. You will get pretty good at knowing when a machine is starting to have issues. Keep oils changed, filters changed, bearings greased, and perform vibration analysis and thermal scanning for hot spots etc...

One area that a supervisor will be expected to keep under control is downtime. Whether it is from machine breakdowns, process flow issues or personnel; downtime will cost a company a lot of money and must be controlled. Review downtime data monthly and prioritize to start to rectify problem areas.

Get involved in the manufacturing process and get to know the costs of key materials. When you see something being wasted and you can drive an issue home with facts, it makes a big difference. If you tell John to not waste so much material you might get a shrug or an ok. If you explain to John that that material costs $2.65 per yard, you might get a better reaction. Let them be part of the solution. If you get employee buy in, you might get some great ideas to save more money. The production employees are the ones that know the process inside and out. Make them part of your continuous improvement teams and Value Stream Map teams.

Remember… watch the pennies, and the dollars will take care of themselves. Spend company money as if it were coming out of your pocket.

CHAPTER SEVEN

GETTING TO THE NEXT LEVEL

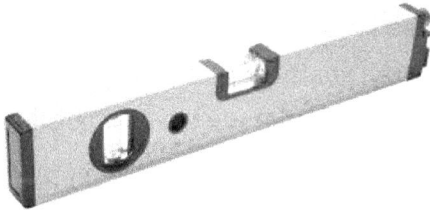

Another one of those buzz word sayings that you hear periodically is "Getting to the next level". What does that mean? Simply put it means going above and beyond. Once you have a certain comfort level, you need to push the boundaries and keep improving. Whether it is getting more organized, taking on a new continuous improvement project or utilizing time management skills; the point is that you need to keep moving forward.

There's always something more that we can be doing. Remember... staying stagnant is the same as moving backwards. Keep moving forward. All companies have goals. Production goals, quality goals etc... All goals need to be adjusted from time to time. Normally that means raising the bar. Even if it's just a little bit, some forward progress is better than none.

Get to know your employees and their personalities. Learn how to motivate each employee as they all have different motivation receptors. Some employees will go a long way with a simple praising for a job well done. Others are motivated by challenges. I have had some employees that would work best if you told them that they couldn't get something accomplished. They just want to prove you wrong.

The best way to get to the next level is to constantly evaluate your employees and coach them through their weaknesses. You need to have good quality team members. Everybody then has to buy into the team philosophy and work together for the common good. Sometimes you will find that you have a great employee but they are performing a job task that they just aren't a good fit for.

You need to be able to recognize this and get that good employee to a job that better suits their talents. I like to use an analogy from the book "Good to Great", written by Jim Collins. Another fantastic book by the way. It's another common sense approach that hits home. You are the bus driver. It's your job to make the stops and get the right people on the bus. Unfortunately, you sometimes have to make some stops and let some people off the bus. Let's just say they are better suited for the subway. The most important part however, is getting the right people on the bus AND getting them in the right seats!

Again, it's unfortunate but you will have employees that just won't or can't be a part of the program. Give them every opportunity and give them all of the tools that they need to succeed. If they still can't help get you to the next level, it's time to let them off the bus.

Here are some simple words to live by and keep in mind when you are trying to get to the next level...

- Have a viable plan – to get to the next level you need to brainstorm. Perform a Value Stream Map or a continuous improvement project. In my opinion, a good committee team should branch off with sub-committees.
- Stay focused – don't start a project and let it die.
- Look in the mirror – you are the quarterback, you need to follow up and make sure you are constantly heading in the right direction. The boat's not going to steer itself!
- Communication – nothing will derail a plan of action like a lack of communication. I said it earlier in the book, the number one reason that a new supervisor will fail is because of a lack of communication.

- Have CLEAR goals – review with the team frequently and make sure that everyone understands the goals and what their role is in achieving the goals.
- Stay the course – don't expect immediate results. If you know that you have a good plan, stick with it. Tweak as needed but give it a chance.
- Recruit advocates – surround yourself as much as you can with people that support you. I know that sounds a little juvenile but it can go a long way.
- Communicate – did I say that already?

The next level will mean different things to different people. For some it may be increasing production by 2%. For others, it might mean reducing quality defects or reducing scrap loss. Sometimes you will discover that reaching one goal will help you reach another goal without even realizing it. For instance, if you found an easier way to boost production that also turned out to be more ergonomic; you just might reduce injuries!

Of course there are two sides to every coin. The other possibility is creating another problem while reaching a goal. Suppose you improve productivity by 3%, but as a result your scrap rate or reject rate has gone up 5%. Not good! Keep an eye on your input and output and how that affects the entire operation. Don't get discouraged. A very good major league baseball player fails two thirds of the time while at bat.

Expect failure. Regroup and keep trying, keep moving forward. Don't be afraid to ask for help. Do what's right and you will be fine.

CHAPTER EIGHT

HIRING, MOTIVATING AND SEPERATION

Still, one of the worst parts of my job is terminating an employee. You would think that after many, many years it would get a little easier. I guess I should be glad that it doesn't. I have to remember that we don't fire people...they fire themselves. It's never comfortable to take away somebody's livelihood and put a burden on their families. That's why I try to give every employee the tools that they need to be successful. Coaching and counseling will only get you so far.

A good Human Resources department can be a supervisor's best friend. It's very important to take the time to research and test all potential candidates. It's very easy to get caught up in just needing a body because you are so shorthanded. You will get much better employees if you take the time and fully research them, do in depth interviews and test them. Safety testing is critical. The last thing that you want is somebody in your production area that doesn't work safely.

You can find other aptitude, personality and skill tests that can be very beneficial. Take the time and take advantage of the opportunity. You will be glad down the road that you invested in them.

Another idea that can be helpful is taking resume's form your trusted employees. Try to sift through the applicants that were just a family member or friend needing a job compared to a good candidate with a proven track record that your employee is willing to put his name on and personally vouch for.

Once you have the right employees, keep them motivated. Believe it or not, most employees want to stay busy and productive. Make sure that everyone stays busy and effective. Pay is of course a huge motivator but there are many other things that you can do within your control.

Again, not to over simplify but a lot of this is common sense. Treat people like you would like to be treated. Most people always like to hear that they are doing a great job.

- ❖ Listen – truly listen to what your employees are telling you and respond in a positive way.
- ❖ Tell them when they are doing a good job and let them know that it's greatly appreciated.
- ❖ Tell them when they aren't doing a good job in a constructive way and tell them how they can do better and offer any help or tools that they need to do better. Again, let

them know that they are appreciated; they are just a little off course.

- ❖ If your company will allow it, have small denomination gift cards or sporting event tickets on hand for when somebody goes above and beyond. I have actually talked to employees and pulled out my wallet and given them a $20 bill and said thank you for making my job easier. You have no idea how much your efforts are appreciated. When they see you are pulling your own money out of your pocket; that really makes an impact. Of course you can't do this very often or you will be looking for a part time job!

- ❖ Let them be leaders of a project or committee. Taking ownership and responsibility will bring pride and motivation to a lot of people.

- ❖ Lead by example. If a particular area is very busy and you can do it, get your hands dirty and lend a hand. Sometimes the little things make a difference. I will pick up a paper off the floor if I see one, I will put down floor dry or sweep if needed. I'm no better than anyone else; we are all on the same team with the same goals.

Finally, when the unfortunate task is upon you and you have an employee that just isn't cutting it start a plan in motion to get them up to speed or cut them loose. The most important thing is to document. Documentation and having them sign it is extremely important. You never know when you will find yourself in court defending your company over something ridiculous. People are suing for frivolous reasons that are unjustified. Unfortunately some people abuse the system hoping a company will want to save money and settle out of court.

Make sure that you spell out specifically why they are not performing to the company standards. Have a time line written so that they understand there must be improvement in 30 days. (Or whatever timeline) Make sure they sign off that they understand and they also understand if they do not improve, they will be subject to termination.

Most people understand and see it coming Never make it personal, because it never is or it never should be. It's just business. Not everybody is good at everything. Sometimes it's just not a good fit. Sometimes people just expect to get paid for nothing and will do nothing but complain constantly. Give them the tools and hold them accountable. Everything will work its way out. Remember... we don't ever fire anybody. They fire themselves.

Ultimately, why would we ever want to fire anyone? There are way too many costs associated with hiring and training a new employee. Not to mention the countless hours of somebody's time.

CHAPTER NINE

LEAN MANUFACTURING

A lot of companies have adapted to a Lean Manufacturing culture. Lean is just a system to improve your processes in a systematic way. Really this has been practiced for decades. Henry Ford was one of the innovators for improving productivity and reducing costs. He declared that the longer an article is in process and moved about, the greater the ultimate cost.

The definition of LEAN is a system to identify and eliminate waste through continuous improvement. There are value added and non-value added activities in every process. Obviously, anything value added increases the market value and the customer is willing to pay for. Non value added steps need to be eliminated or reduced as they do not add value to the product and the customer is not willing to pay for them.

In a sense, it is all about eliminating waste and improving the flow. Lean is all about keeping it simple and visual. Breaking things down step by step with visuals aids. There are eight wastes in manufacturing; I like to use the Acronym DOWNTIME to help remember them...

Defects

Overproduction

Waiting

Non Value Added processing

Transportation

Inventory (excess)

Movement

Employee underutilization

A good lean tool to start with is "5S". This is simply cleaning and organizing. "5S" stands for SORT, SET IN ORDER, SHINE, STANDARDIZE and SUSTAIN. Shadow boards, racks, color coding, and shelving are all great tools to be used in a "5S" project. Start with a marked area to place items that don't seem to have a home. If it doesn't get used, you probably need to get rid of it. Don't let things that don't belong clutter up the work area.

To improve productivity, a lot of time should be spent studying the process. It is important to understand how much time each step of the process takes. This is where brainstorming ideas come from. Ideas like automatic inspection or measurement can significantly reduce process time. Sometimes just rearranging the flow can make a world of difference. Sometimes it takes a significant amount of capital to upgrade the production unit, but many times the return on investment can be pretty quick.

I have talked a little about Value Stream Maps. A VSM is a simple visual approach to mapping out your process. Start to finish, you point out each step and break down how long each step takes. You start with a current state map and show the process as it is currently. For instance if you had to make hamburgers...

You would need cell stations with supplies for the entire process. Cell one puts down a plate, cell two puts a bun on the plate, cell three puts a burger on the bun, cell four puts a piece of lettuce on the burger, cell five puts a tomato on and finally cell six wraps it and puts it in a bag. You need to make sure that each cell doesn't run out of inventory.

Next, you need to know your demand and figure out your cycle time. Let's assume each process takes 10 seconds for simplicity. Once you are started, you should have a hamburger off the line every 10 seconds. If you discovered that you had a bottleneck and it takes 20 seconds to wrap the burger and put it in a bag, you could have cell six just wrap the burger and add another cell to put it in a bag. Of course if it only takes five seconds to put on a tomato and 5 seconds to put on lettuce, you could combine the two cells.

It's all about streamlining the process and producing the right amount of material at the right frequency. Sometimes you can never seem to meet demand. You have to keep reviewing and performing VSM exercises until you get the desired results. It's really not about making people work harder. It's about working smarter and more efficient and getting the tools needed to perform the job in the most effective way.

After you map your process with a current state map, you will want to make a future state map. This is how you want the process to be in the amount of time desired. You might show only three cells in the future or maybe extend to eight cells. It all depends on the amount of material needed in a desired timeframe.

Busters Burgers Value Stream Map – Current State

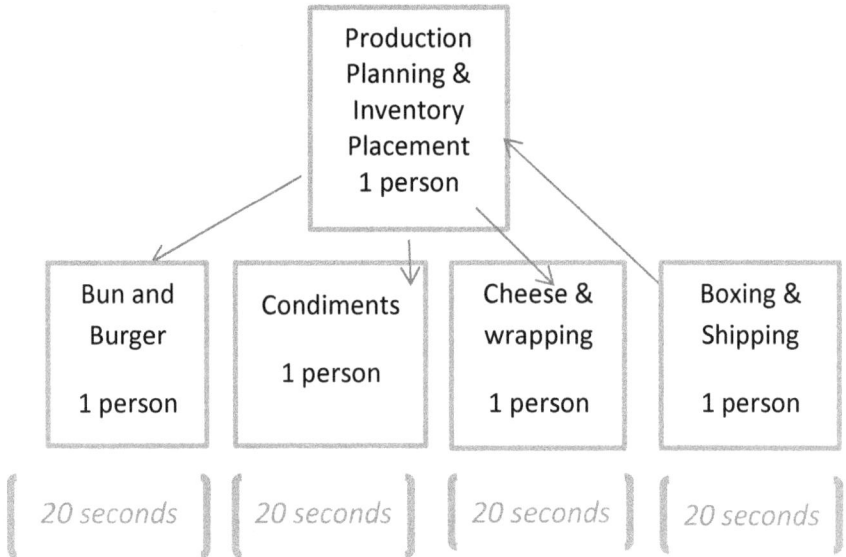

Production Planning & Inventory Placement 1 person

Bun and Burger 1 person	Condiments 1 person	Cheese & wrapping 1 person	Boxing & Shipping 1 person
20 seconds	*20 seconds*	*20 seconds*	*20 seconds*

It takes 5 people to make and wrap a burger in 20 seconds. (Once the line is full) So we can produce 180 burgers in an hour. This means we can produce roughly 1440 burgers per day. What if we received a new order of an additional 1440 burgers a day? We could start a second shift, or maybe add just two people and tweak the process...

Busters Burgers Value Stream Map – Future State

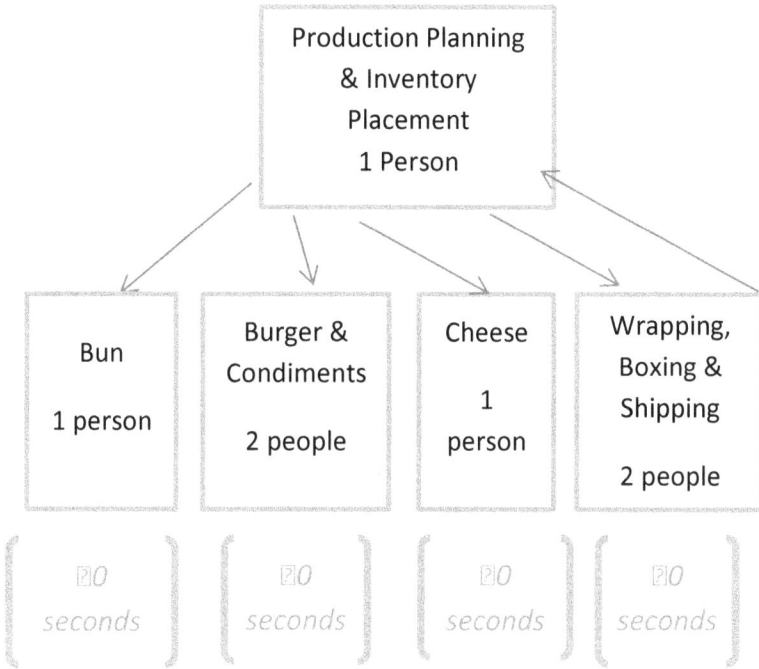

```
                    ┌─────────────────────┐
                    │  Production Planning │
                    │     & Inventory      │
                    │      Placement       │
                    │      1 Person        │
                    └─────────────────────┘
```

Bun	Burger & Condiments	Cheese	Wrapping, Boxing & Shipping
1 person	2 people	1 person	2 people
⯑0 seconds	⯑0 seconds	⯑0 seconds	⯑0 seconds

Now, it takes 7 people to make and wrap a burger in 10 seconds. (Once the line is full) So we can produce 360 burgers in an hour. This means we can now produce roughly 2880 burgers per day.

CHAPTER TEN

PROBLEM SOLVING AND ROOT CAUSE ANALYSIS

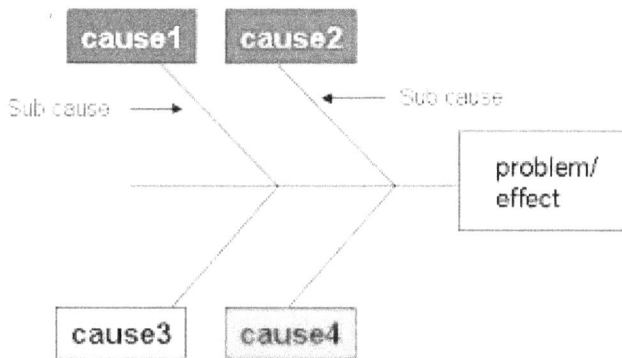

Never underestimate the importance of problem solving. Every good supervisor must be able to solve problems. That's really what a supervisor is paid to do. Communicate in all directions and make decisions. Some of the tougher decisions require a lot of thought and sometimes a lot of time. The only way that you can solve a serious problem is to truly understand the problem. That's the most important step.

The best way to understand the problem is to break it down into small sections. I like to break it down into four possible root cause scenarios. MAN, METHOD MATERIAL OR MACHINE.

MAN – This breaks the problem down to investigate any possibility that the problem is caused by a person. An S.O.P. may not be followed correctly, somebody maybe didn't understand what they were supposed to do, or simply the individual is not capable or competent enough to perform the desired task.

METHOD – This is where you need to review how the task is performed and the work instructions that spell out how to perform the task. Maybe something has changed since the work instructions were written. Possibly, the work instructions were never accurate but the individual performing the task "adjusted" and made the process work. Of course if the changes were not documented, the next person to perform the task would have the same issues and find their way to "adjust."

MATERIAL – Obviously the product or raw materials that we are using such as steel, plastic, or wood. Are there defects or variation in the dimensions? Is the surface and shape quality good?

MACHINE – Finally, the machine itself needs to be scrutinized. Did something change? Maybe a bearing or shaft has worn and the machine is not running exactly as it used to. Maybe something has come out of alignment.

   Sometimes it can take days to really dig deep into a problem and find the root cause or causes. By taking each category and drilling down, you will find a potential root cause and probably other smaller issues that you were not even aware of. Often times, teams can find ways to improve a process when they start dissecting it down to solve a problem.

EXAMPLE: Super Paint Co. is painting 16" wide coil steel. The process is to un-wind the coil, clean it in a bath of water and sodium hydroxide solution, rinse it with fresh heated water, dry the steel in an industrial dryer with edge spray from compressed air, paint the steel with an automated quick dry spray paint, pass through a bake oven and re-wrap the coil.

THE PROBLEM – Every now and then a customer complains that parts of his steel are not painted or they get what appears to be a smear mark. It never lasts for a long time, but it's a nuisance none the less. Management has discovered that every defect can be traced back to your shift.

LET'S BREAK IT DOWN:

MAN -

- There are no new operators in the past year.
- No temporary workers have been assigned to cover vacations or medical leave.
- There is no reason to believe any employee is disgruntled or any reason to suspect sabotage.

- All of the operators have been questioned and agree that nobody has changed the process in any way.
- The only new employees hired in the past year were a maintenance technician and a shipping clerk, both now on your shift.
- There were no supervisor changes or vacation coverage in the past six months.

MACHINE -

- The wash section and rinse section were inspected thoroughly for concentration, spray, temperature; etc... all seems to be fine.
- The spray booth and headers have all been inspected, everything is working correctly.
- The paint used has been verified to be the same as always used.
- The dryer section, velocity, flow, header angles are all fine.
- The edge blow off seems to be working fine as well with plenty of flow and the right blow off angle.
- The entire line was inspected for the possibility of grease, debris or hydraulic

fluid dropping onto the strip. – Nothing found.

- The air compressor dryer is working fine and we are not getting any condensation in the air line after the strip dryer.

MATERIAL –

- The material was thoroughly checked and rechecked to be in specification completely.

METHOD -

- All work instructions and process flow diagrams have been reviewed and verified.
- No new steps have been added or deleted to S.O.P.'s.
- Since the problem was identified, more data has shown the issue oddly enough can be traced back to material ran between 3:30 pm and 5:00 pm.
- More data gathered has proven that the issue is always on the bottom side edges.

With the above data it was decided to staff extra bodies throughout the line concentrating on the strip coming out of the dryer and directly after applying the paint. It was quickly discovered that at around 4pm there were slightly wet edges on the bottom edges of the strip before painting. After many people scrambling to figure out what was going on, the problem cleared up after a few minutes and did not return the rest of the shift.

Day two presented almost the exact same scenario at about 4:15 pm and again lasted only a few minutes. It was proven that the edge blow offs had lost a significant amount of pressure for a few minutes. Going back to our fishbone diagram and root cause analysis, we recognized that there was a new maintenance tech hired in the past few months. When the team broke down the issue again with the remaining factors, the maintenance man was interviewed and asked if he was doing anything routinely every day around 4pm. He said no, not really. After a pause, then said, "Oh, I do blow down the compressor every day around 4pm".

The supervisor asked him to show how and what he was doing. The tech was not following the instructions that he was taught. He was told to crack the blow down valve no more than ¼ of the way for about 2 minutes. He said that he figured it was quicker to open the valve 100% open for 30 seconds. This caused too much drain on the tank and reduced the flow and velocity just enough to leave a little bit of a wet edge on the strip. In turn, the paint would not stick to the strip if it were damp.

PROBLEM SOLVED....

You can't stop there! You need to make sure that this NEVER happens again. The team hung a sign to not crack the blow down valve for more than 2 minutes at a maximum of ¼" open. They also updated the work instructions and FMEA. The team felt good and presented the plan to the Plant Manager who was very happy with one exception. He congratulated the team on a job well done. Now, let's take it one step further. How do we make sure another new employee doesn't follow the same path? The better solution was to install an automatic blow down device that blew the compressor down every day at 6am at a very slow rate for two minutes. NOW, the problem is solved. Of course the automatic blow down has to be inspected on a regular basis.

CHAPTER ELEVEN

PRACTICE AND LEAD BY EXAMPLE

Well, I certainly hope that this book has been useful and helpful. Don't sweat the little things but put your time and effort into the important things. Don't be a boss, be a leader and lead by example. Follow up; your employees want to be able to count on you. Build that trust and respect. Don't ever think that you deserve respect just because of your title, you don't!

The only way to win respect is by leading by example. Walk the walk and talk the talk. I guarantee you will constantly be watched and judged, and that's ok. If you are thin skinned or worry about what others are saying, you won't make a good supervisor. Show them! Be a leader.

Remember the basics...

- Safety FIRST
- Care about what you are doing and the people that are helping you get there
- Treat others as you want to be treated
- Be fair and consistent
- Listen, really listen. Practice effectively listening

- Communicate often and effectively
- Lead by example
- Say what you do, do what you say
- Surround yourself with people that support you
- Don't succumb to office politics, rumors and gossip
- Follow up
- Never discipline in front of others
- Try to have fun and make work fun
- When you wake up one morning and hate to go into work, it's time to move on. Nobody should hate waking up every morning.
- Don't abuse your power or let it go to your head

www.ingramcontent.com/pod-product-compliance
Lightning Source LLC
Chambersburg PA
CBHW060644210326
41520CB00010B/1727